THE WONDERFUL WORLD OF WORDS

6

Prince Pronoun Gets into Trouble

Dr Lubna Alsagoff

PhD (Stanford)

 **Marshall Cavendish**
Children

King Noun was a very busy
man — he was sometimes not
around to do all the things he
had to do in the kingdom.

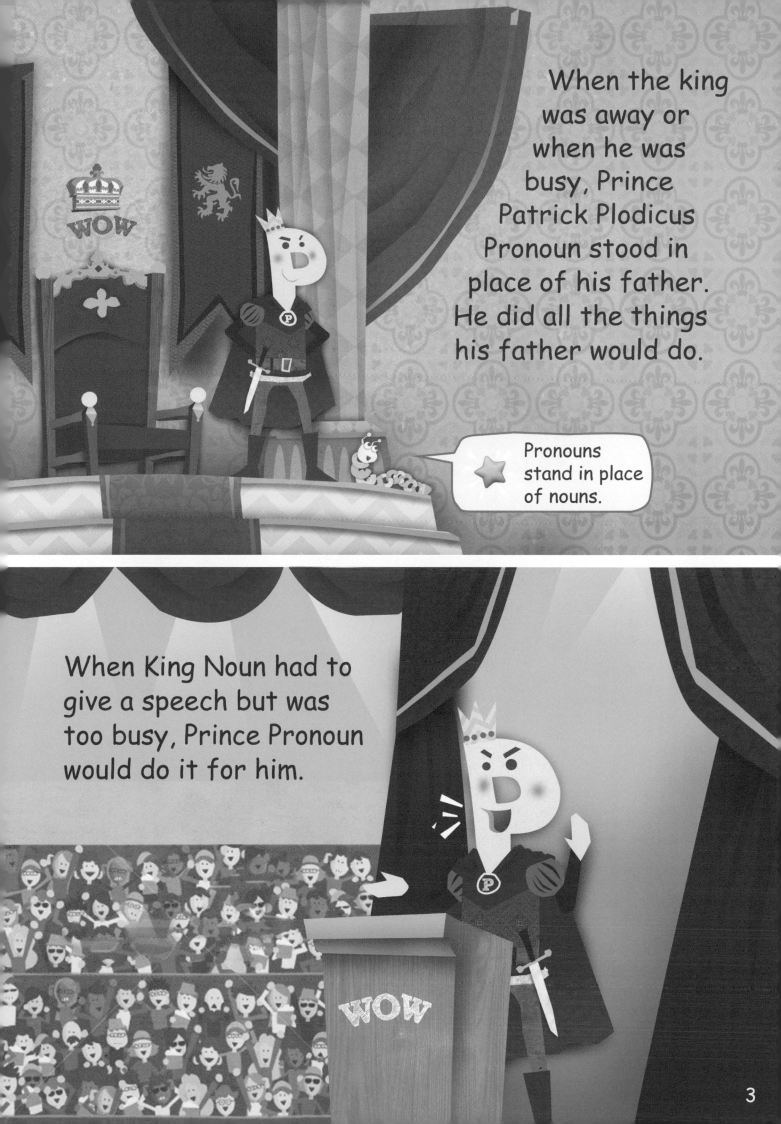

When the king was away or when he was busy, Prince Patrick Plodicus Pronoun stood in place of his father. He did all the things his father would do.

Pronouns stand in place of nouns.

When King Noun had to give a speech but was too busy, Prince Pronoun would do it for him.

3

The prince also listened to the people of WOW who needed help when the king was away.

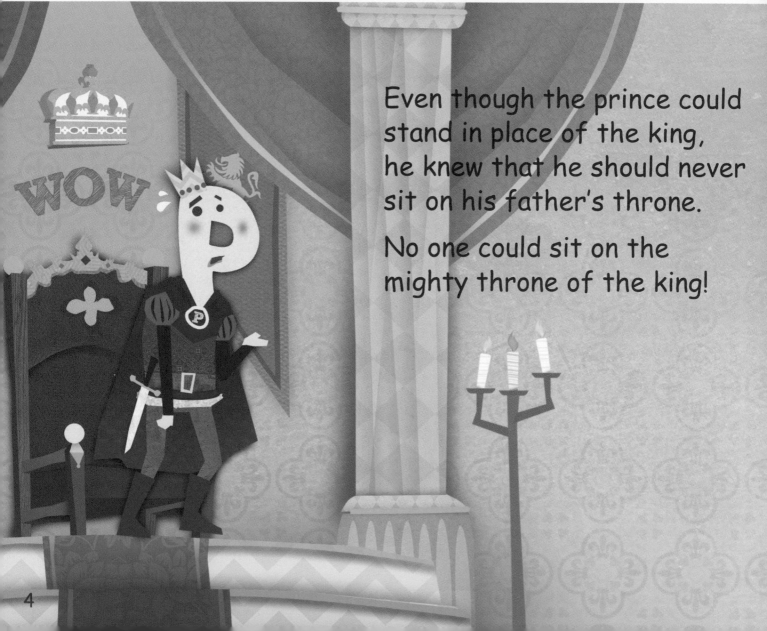

Even though the prince could stand in place of the king, he knew that he should never sit on his father's throne.

No one could sit on the mighty throne of the king!

One day, however, the young prince grew very tired.

And before he knew it, he fell fast asleep on his father's throne.

The king saw the prince sitting on his throne and became very angry.

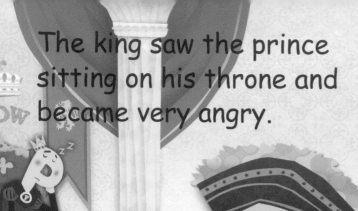

How dare you sit on my throne! You are not the king of WOW.

I'm very sorry, Father. I was just so very tired.

But King Noun was very upset.

Guards, take the prince to the dungeon!

The queen immediately summoned the editor of the WOW Times, the kingdom's newspaper.

She told the editor her idea.

Ah!

The next morning, King Noun read the newspaper as he was eating breakfast. But, something was wrong!

There is something terribly wrong with the WOW Times today!

Really? There's nothing wrong with my copy of the newspaper!

Can you circle the differences between the king's and queen's copies of the newspaper to find out what's wrong with the king's?

A New School Opens in WOW

Yesterday morning, the citizens of WOW watched as King Norman Nautilus Noun, ruler of the great kingdom of WOW, officially opened Claridge Primary School.

After King Noun cut the ribbon, King Noun gave a speech. King Noun told the people of WOW how much King Noun loved going to school.

King Noun said that King Noun was happy to have been invited to open the school.

A New School Opens in WOW

Yesterday morning, the citizens of WOW watched as King Norman Nautilus Noun, ruler of the great kingdom of WOW, officially opened Claridge Primary School.

After King Noun cut the ribbon, he gave a speech. He told the people of WOW how much he loved going to school.

King Noun said that he was happy to have been invited to open the school.

King Noun now saw the problem.

My copy of the newspaper has no pronouns! No wonder it sounds so strange!

Yes, pronouns take the place of nouns. When pronouns are not around, the nouns must be repeated over and over.

Yes, when I'm not around...

...Prince Pronoun does your work!

Can you fill in the right pronouns for the different people and things?

King Noun

_____ loves going for long walks.
The people of WOW respect _____.

Queen Verb

_____ has a shiny, new car.
The people of WOW admire _____.

Artisan Adverb and
Admiral Adjective

_____ are very good friends.
The king and queen depend on _____.

Queen Verb's car

_____ is a beautiful car!
The queen loves to drive
_____ all over WOW.

14

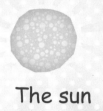

The sun

_____ is shining very brightly today. You must not look directly at _____.

The school

_____ is a new school. Many students will attend _____ next year.

The people of WOW

_____ live happily in the kingdom of WOW. The king and queen visit _____.

The WOW cat

_____ lives in the WOW castle. The WOW family feed _____ delicious sardines.

The Fabulous Forest of WOW

Owl, Rabbit and Squirrel were thinking about what Donkey told them.

The animals began to speak strangely after the purple cloud appeared.

Suddenly, they see Magpie falling from the sky!

She lands with a thump on the grass patch near them. Next to her is a very big book.

Oh my! What happened?

I think it's Magpie. And look! She has a book with her.

18

19

All this time, Magpie was not listening to what Owl, Rabbit and Squirrel were saying. She was still looking for something.

Owl, Rabbit and Squirrel wanted to learn how to cure the animals.

Owl, Rabbit and Squirrel started to learn about the different types of words.

ADVERB NOUN
ARTICLE VERB
PRONOUN
ADJECTIVE

VERB + ING

VERB : wait

I am _ _ _ _ _ _ _ _ _.

He is _ _ _ _ _ _ _ _.

They are _ _ _ _ _ _ _ _.

VERB : pick

I am _ _ _ _ _ _ _ _.

He is _ _ _ _ _ _ _ _.

They are _ _ _ _ _ _ _ _.

VERB : jump

I am _ _ _ _ _ _ _ _.

He is _ _ _ _ _ _ _ _.

They are _ _ _ _ _ _ _ _.

VERB : walk

I am _ _ _ _ _ _ _ _.

She is_ _ _ _ _ _ _ _ _ .

They are _ _ _ _ _ _ _ _.

VERB : call

I am _ _ _ _ _ _ _ _.

She is _ _ _ _ _ _ _ _.

They are _ _ _ _ _ _ _ _.

VERB + ED

wait _ _ _ _ _ _ _

jump _ _ _ _ _ _

walk _ _ _ _ _ _

pick _ _ _ _ _ _

call _ _ _ _ _ _ _

I hope that we will be able to help the animals get better!

Owl, Rabbit and Squirrel were so happy that they finally found out what was wrong with the animals.

Dear Parents,

In this issue, children should notice and learn two areas of grammar.

- Children should notice how pronouns are used in the place of nouns where we don't need to repeat the nouns. Children should know which pronouns to use with male, female, one (singular) or many (plural) persons. There are also two pronouns, e.g., for the male, singular pronoun: *he* and *him*. We'll learn about that in later volumes.

- We also learn more about the **ed** and **ing** word endings that some verbs need. Children should see that the **ing** form comes after **is**, **are** or **am**.

Page	Possible Answers
14–15	King Noun: he | him Queen Verb: she | her Artisan Adverb and Admiral Adjective: they | them Queen Verb's car: it | it The sun: it | it The school: it | it The people of WOW: they | them The WOW cat: it | it
22	I am waiting | picking | jumping | walking | calling He is waiting | picking | jumping | walking | calling They are waiting | picking | jumping | walking | calling
23	waited | jumped | walked | picked | called